Right of Petition.

NEW ENGLAND CLERGYMEN.

REMARKS

OF

MESSRS. EVERETT,	MESSRS. DOUGLAS,	MESSRS. HOUSTON,
" MASON,	" BUTLER,	" ADAMS,
" PETTIT,	" SEWARD,	" BADGER.

ON THE

MEMORIAL

FROM SOME 3,050 CLERGYMEN OF ALL DENOMINATIONS AND SECTS IN THE DIFFERENT STATES IN NEW ENGLAND, REMONSTRATING AGAINST THE PASSAGE OF THE NEBRASKA BILL.

SENATE OF THE UNITED STATES, MARCH 14, 1854.

WASHINGTON, D. C.
BUELL & BLANCHARD, PRINTERS.
1854.

STEREOTYPED AT THE
BALTIMORE TYPE AND STEREOTYPE FOUNDRY,
LUCAS BROTHERS, PROPRIETORS.

RIGHT OF PETITION.

IN SENATE.

TUESDAY, March 14, 1854.

MR. EVERETT, presented a memorial from some three thousand and fifty clergymen of all denominations and sects in the different States in New England, remonstrating against the passage of the Nebraska bill.

The memorial, on the motion of Mr. EVERETT, having been laid upon the table,

Mr. DOUGLAS subsequently rose and said: A memorial has been ordered to lie on the table, which was presented a few minutes ago by the honorable Senator from Massachusetts, [Mr. EVERETT.] I desire to submit a word or two of comment upon it, and therefore I wish to have it read. I think it is not respectful to the Senate.

The PRESIDENT. The Senator from Illinois moves to take up the memorial which was ordered to lie on the table.

The motion was agreed to.

Mr. DOUGLAS. I would now like to have the memorial read.

It was read, as follows:

To the Honorable the Senate and House of Representatives, in Congress assembled:

The undersigned, clergymen of different religious denominations in New England, hereby, in the name of Almighty God, and in his presence, do solemnly protest against the passage of what is known as the Nebraska bill, or any repeal or modification of the existing legal prohibitions of slavery in that part of our national domain which it is proposed to organize into the territories of Nebraska and Kanzas. We protest against it as a great moral wrong, as a breach of faith eminently unjust to the moral principles of the community, and subversive of all confidence in national engagements; as a measure full of danger to the peace and even the existence of our beloved Union, and exposing us to the righteous judgments of the Almighty: and your protestants, as in duty bound, will ever pray.

Boston, Massachusetts, March 1, 1854.

Mr. DOUGLAS. My only object is to call the attention of the Senate to the memorial. It is presented, after the final vote of the Senate, as a protest against our action—against the action in which largely more than two-thirds of this body concurred. It protests against our action as being a breach of faith, as involving a moral wrong, as destructive of all confidence, and as subjecting us to the righteous judgment of the Almighty. It is presented, too, by a denomination of men calling themselves preachers of the Gospel. Sir, it has been demonstrated in debate that there is not a particle of truth in the allegation of a breach of faith or breach of confidence. It has been demonstrated so clearly, that there is no excuse for any man in the community for believing it any longer. Yet, here we find that a large body of preachers, perhaps three thousand, following the lead of a circular, which was issued by the Abolition confederates in this body, calculated to deceive and mislead the public, have here come forward, with an atrocious falsehood and an atrocious calumny against this Senate, desecrated the pulpit, and prostituted the sacred desk to the miserable and corrupting influence of party politics. It matters not whether the description is confined to narrow limits, or whether it extends to all the clergymen of New England. It matters not whether the misrepresentation has taken a broad scope, or been confined to a few; I hold it as our duty to expose the conduct of men who, under the cloak of religion, either from ignorance or wilful misrepresentation, will avail themselves of their sacred calling to arraign the conduct of Senators here in the discharge of our duties. Sir, I hold that this Senate is as capable of judging whether our action involves moral turpitude, whether it involves the subversion of morals, whether it subjects us to the judgment of the Almighty, as are these political preachers, whose protest proves them to be without any reliable information upon the subject. It is evident, sir, that these men know not what they are talking about. It is evident that they ought to be rebuked, and required to confine themselves to their vocation, instead of neglecting their flocks, and bringing our holy religion into disrepute by violating its sacred principles, and disregarding the obligations of truth and honor, by presenting here a document which is so offensive that no gentleman can indorse it without violating all the rules of courtesy, of propriety, and of honor.

Sir, there seems to be an attempt to pile upon our table offensive document after offensive document, slander after slander, libel after libel, in order that the Abolition press may copy it as coming from the records of the Senate, and go back and give it credit in the country. They are smuggled in here, the offensive matter concealed from our knowledge until we happen to look into them and see what they are, and then these gentlemen expect to carry on a political campaign by quoting from our own records that we are traitors to our country, traitors to God, and traitors to humanity. I think it is time that this miserable system of electioneering by violating the rules and courtesies of the Senate, to get an indorsement of libels, which men ought to be ashamed to adopt, should be exposed and rebuked. I am not willing that they should be permitted to pile up slander of that kind, insult of that kind, upon our table, and let it then be used for such a purpose. You know, sir, that that memorial is not intended to affect the action of the Senate. We have no such bill before us. Our action is passed. It is not for the purpose of influencing our official conduct. Why is it brought here? There can be no other object in presenting it here now than simply to furnish capital for organizing a great sectional party, and trying to draw the whole religious community into their schemes of political aggrandizement. I think that men ought to be able to rely upon argument, and upon truth, and upon reason, instead of resorting to these things for the purpose of stimulating excitement for political ends. I have no motion to submit, but I felt it to be my duty to call the attention of the Senate to the memorial.

Mr. HOUSTON. I think that a petition of this kind ought to be received, and that it is not subject to the charge brought against it by the Senator from Illinois. It does not arraign our action by being drawn up after that action was had. The Nebraska bill passed this body on the night of the 3d, or rather on the morning of the 4th instant. The memorial appears to be dated on the 1st of March. I cannot think that it meant any indignity to the Senate. There is nothing expressive of any such feeling in it. It is a right that all individuals in the community have, if their terms are respectful, to memorialize the Senate of the United States upon any subject. Whether there is any ulterior object in this, I know not; but from the date of the memorial, and from the number of signers, I am induced to believe that the memorialists thought there was something wrong in that bill; and if they believed that its passage would be a breach of faith on the part of the Government, they had a right to say so. I took the liberty of making the same charge here. There were more questions than that of non-intervention involved in that bill. It involved an infraction of faith with the Indians, of pledges given to them under all the solemn forms, yet mockery, of treaties. That was one point involved; and I charged that the passage of the bill would be a violation of plighted faith in that particular. Was it a violation of faith to disregard the Missouri compromise, which was of so much antiquity and utility to the country? That is a matter of discussion. I have not arraigned the action of any gentleman since the passage of the bill, but anterior to it I gave my opinions in relation to its character, as a disregard of treaties, and as a flagrant violation of the plighted faith of the nation towards the Indians. With respect to the Missouri compromise, I believe its repeal to be as flagrant a breach of faith as the violation of treaties made with the Indians.

I have not charged Senators with corrupt motives, nor have I charged them with anything selfish; but I certainly can see no more impropriety in ministers of the Gospel, in their vocation, memorializing Congress, than politicians, or other individuals. I do not believe that these ministers have sent this memorial here to manufacture political capital, to have it entered on the records of the Senate, so that it might be taken back and disseminated through the country. Sir, it comes from the country. I told you that there would be agitation; but it was denied upon this floor. Is not this agitation? Three thousand ministers of the living God upon earth—his vicegerents—send a memorial here upon this subject; and yet you tell me that there is no excitement in the country! Sir, you realize what I anticipated. The country has to bear the infliction.

Sir, the *coup d'état* was not successful. The bill did not pass before the community was awakened to it. The community was awakened to it not alone in New England, for I have seen letters from the south and west stating that it was there regarded as a breach of faith; and I can see no wrong in ministers expressing their opinion in regard to it. This protest does not attack the reputation of Senators. It does not displace them from their positions here. It does not impair their capabilities for the discharge of the high functions which the Constitution has devolved upon them. I see nothing wrong in all this. Ministers have a right to remonstrate. They are like other men. Because they are ministers of the Gospel they are not disfranchised of political rights and privileges; and, if their language is respectful to the Senate, in anticipation of the passage of a bill which was obnoxious to them, they have a right to spread their opinions on the records of the nation. The great national heart throbs under this measure; its pulse beats high; and is it surprising that we should observe the effects of it? I trust, sir, that the nation may yet again see the blessed tranquillity that prevailed over the whole country when this "healing measure" was introduced into the Senate. The nation's position was enviable. It was unagitated. There was not, in my recollection, a time so tranquil and a community more happy. A nation more prosperous existed not upon the earth. Sir, I trust that there will be no continuance of agitation; but the way to end it is not to make war upon memorialists. Let them memorialize if they think it necessary. If they state what is incorrect, let the subject be referred to committees, and let the committees give an exposition of the truth, and lay it, in reports, before the public, and then the intelligence of the nation will determine as to what is right, and what consideration ought to be given to it. I would not take away the liberty to indulge in the freest expression of opinion, or the exercise of the rights and privileges which belong to any portion of this country; yet I would discourage agitation. I may hold the contents of this protest, to some extent, heretical; yet they are not expressed in such offensive language as would justify a denial of their right to memorialize. If it had been intended to impugn our motives or our actions, either as corrupt or immoral, we could bear it. The people surely have a right to think and speak upon our action. We are not placed in a position so high that we are elevated above the questioning power of the people. They have the right to look into our action, and investigate our conduct; and, if they do not approve of it, to express their opinions in relation to it. I shall never make war upon them on that account; yet I trust that, whatever disposition may be made of the bill which we have passed, the agitation has already reached its acme; and that from this point it may decline, until the country is again restored to peace and happiness.

Mr. MASON. That it is the right of the citizens of the United States to petition Congress, or either House of it, upon any subject that may be presented to them, is never denied, never should be denied; and such petition upon any subject of public interest should be received and treated with the respect which is due to citizens. I trust I shall never see the day when the Senate of the United States will treat the authors of such petitions, upon any subject proper for legislation pending before the body, coming from the people of the United States with aught but respect. But I understand this petition to come from a class who have put aside their character of citizens. It comes from a class who style themselves in the petition, ministers of the Gospel, and not citizens. They come before us—I have not understood the petition wrong, I believe—as ministers of the Gospel, not citizens, and denounce prospectively the action of the Senate, in their language, as a moral wrong; and they have the temerity, in the presence of the citizens of the United States, to invoke the vengeance of the Almighty, whom they profess to serve, against us. Sir, ministers of the Gospel are unknown to this Government, and God forbid the day should ever come when they shall be known to it. The great effort of the American people has been, by every form of defensive measures, to keep that class away from the Government; to deny to them any access to it as a class, or any interference in its proceedings. The best illustration of the wisdom of that measure in our Government is to be found in this. Ministers of the Gospel, I repeat, are unknown to the Government. Their mission upon earth is unknown to the Government. Of all others, they are the most encroaching, and, as a body, arrogant class of men. What do these ministers say? Do they as citizens, enter into a statement of the facts of which they complain? Do they recite what will be the political effects of the measure which they complain? No; they inform us that they come here, through their petition, in the presence of the Almighty, and invoke His vengeance upon the Senate of the United States as about to commit, in their judgment, a great moral wrong.

Now, sir, I am perfectly willing to let any number of citizens protest against the measure which has recently passed the Senate. They have a right to do so, in respectful language, such as becomes gentlemen in addressing each other. If thirty thousand, or three hundred thousand citizens come from New England, let them be heard. It is a respect due to them; but when they come here, not as citizens, but declaring that they come as ministers of the Gospel, and, as the honorable Senator from Texas declared them to be, vicegerents of the Almighty—so I understood him to declare, possibly he meant vice-regents to supervise and control the legislation of the country—I say, when they come here as a class unknown to the Government, a class that the Government does not mean to know in any form or shape, not to recommend or remonstrate, but to denounce our action as a great moral wrong, because they claim to be the "vicegerents" of the Almighty, we are bound—not from disrespect to them as citizens, not from disrespect to the cloth which they do not grace, but from respect to the Government, from respect to that sacred public trust which has been committed to us—to carry out the policy of the Government and refuse to recognize them. Sir, their object, as was well said by the Senator from Illinois, has been agitation—agitation; and I presume that their cloth and their ministry will enable them to agitate with some success. I say, then, Mr. President, in my judgment, it is due to the Government, to the public trust which we are here to administer, that we should carry out the policy of the Government and refuse to recognize these ministers of the Gospel in coming here. I move, therefore, that the petition be not received, as the best evidence of the sense of the Senate of its character.

Mr. BUTLER. It has been received, I believe, and all that is left is to protest against the protestants. I have great respect, Mr. President, for the pulpit. I have such a respect for it that I would almost submit to a rebuke from a minister of the Gospel, even in my official capacity; but they lose a portion of my respect when I see an organization, for, I believe, the first time in the history of this Government, of clergymen within a local precinct, within the limits of New England, assuming to be, as the Senator from Texas said, the vicegerents of Heaven, coming to the Senate of the United States, not as citizens, as my friend from Virginia has said, but as the organs of God—for they do not come here petitioning or presenting their views under the sanction of the obligations and responsibilities of citizens under the Constitution of the United States, but they have dared to quit the pulpit, and step into the political arena, and speak as the organs of Almighty God. Sir, they assume to be the foremen of the jury which is to pronounce the verdict and judgment of God upon earth. They do not protest as ordinary citizens do; but they mingle in their protest what they would have us believe is the judgment of the Almighty. When the clergy quit the province which is assigned to them, in which they can dispense the Gospel—that Gospel which is represented as the lamb, not as the tiger or the lion—when they would convert the lamb into the lion, going about in the form of agitators, seeking whom they may devour, instead of the meek and lowly representatives of Christ, they divest themselves of all respect which I can give them. Sir, the ministers of the Gospel are the representatives of the lowly and poor lamb—of Christ; but when the men who have signed that paper—I do not know with what ends; I do not say a word against them as individuals, for I have no doubt they are good and respectable, and many of them Christians—assume to organize themselves as clergymen to come before the country and protest against the deliberations of the Senate of the United States, they deserve, at least, the grave censure of the body.

Mr. ADAMS. During the discussion of the Nebraska bill before the Senate I did not open my mouth; nor should I now but for the remarks which have fallen from the distinguished Senator from Texas, my old and familiar friend. He says there is agitation, and that the display upon your table is evidence of it. Suppose there is agitation; at whose door ought the fault to lie, if there be fault? Was the action of this body right or wrong? If we did what was right and proper, according to the republican institutions of this country, and agitation arises out of it, the responsibility neither rests upon the distinguished Senator who introduced the bill nor those who voted for it. What was that action? This body, by its vote, removed a legislative censure upon the institutions of the South—a censure which has existed for more than thirty years, and under which we had lived submissively until now for the sake of peace. For the first time in thirty years, when that censure could be repealed, when the southern States place themselves as the Constitution places them, upon an equality with the northern States, we are committing a very great outrage when we simply say that the people of every portion of this country within the limits of our Constitutional authority, shall be governed by their own laws in their own way. That is the whole of it.

I concur with my friend from South Carolina in regard to the petition which has been presented and ordered to lie on the table. It is addressed to the Senate and House of Representatives by a body of individuals as ministers of the Gospel. I trust I have as high a regard for their vocation as any other individual, and as much respect for the ministers of peace and good will on earth as any other individual; but when they depart from their high vocation, and come down to mingle in the turbid pools of politics, I would treat them just as I would all other citizens. I would treat their memorials and remonstrances precisely as I would those of other citizens. It is so unlike the apostles and the ministers of Christ at an early day, that it loses the potency which they suppose the styling themselves ministers of the Gospel would give to their memorials. The early ministers of Christ attended to their mission, one which was given to them by their Master; and under all circumstances, even when the Saviour himself was upon earth, and attempts were made to induce him to give opinions with reference to the municipal affairs of the Government, he refused. These men have descended from their high estate to assail the action of this body. The Senator from Massachusetts, in presenting the petition, has done what he considered to be his duty; but I would remark, however, that with all the respect which belongs to the high character of those individuals as ministers of the Gospel, their petition should, under the circumstances, receive no more respect from us than if it came from any other private citizens.

Mr. HOUSTON. Mr. President, I have the misfortune again to differ from my friends in relation to this measure, but that difference is not sufficient to induce me to enter anew into the discussion of it. I will, however, discuss the propriety of this memorial. The gentlemen misapprehend its character entirely. I understood the honorable Senator from Virginia—but I may have been mistaken—to say that it invoked the vengeance of the Almighty God upon the Senate.

Mr. MASON. In substance it does, as I understand.

Mr. HOUSTON. There is no invocation contained in the memorial. It is a respectful protest, stating their appreciation of the measure then pending before the Senate of the United States, and not one word is contained in it derogatory to the Senate at the time it was drawn, and there is no invocation of wrath or vengeance upon the members of this body. It is a respectful protest, in the name of the Almighty God.

By the expression which I used when I was up before, that they were the vicegerents of the Almighty, I merely intended to say that they were harbingers of peace to their fellow men; and if it was a *lapsus linguæ*, or improper expression, it does not change the intention that I then entertained in my mind, of expressing a belief that it was nothing else than an extraordinary emergency that diverted men from their ordinary pursuits in the ministry of the Gospel to engage at all in, or to step even to the verge of, the political arena.

We are told, Mr. President, that this was intended for the purpose of agitation. It is certainly a manifestation of agitation; but it could not have been intended to create agitation, for the thing was done, and here is one of its developments and consequences. Yet, sir, I can see nothing wrong in the memorial, so far as I am concerned. If ministers of the Gospel are not recognized by the Constitution of the United States, they are recognized by the moral and social constitution of society. They are recognized in the constitution of man's salvation. The great Redeemer of the world enjoined duties upon mankind; and there is the moral constitution from which we have derived all the excellent principles of our political constitution—the great principles upon which our Government, morally, socially, and religiously, is founded.

Then, sir, I do not think there is anything very derogatory to our institutions in the ministers of the Gospel expressing their opinions. They have a right to do it. No man can be a minister without first being a man. He has political rights; he has also the rights of a missionary of the Saviour, and he is not disfranchised by his vocation. Certain political restrictions may be laid upon him; he may be disqualified from serving in the legislatures of the States, but that does not discharge him from political and civil obligations to his country. He has a right to contribute, as far as he thinks necessary, to the sustentation of its institutions. He has a right to interpose his voice as one of its citizens against the adoption of any measure which he believes will injure the nation. These individuals have done no more. They have not denounced the Senate, but they have protested, in the capacity of ministers, against what I and other Senators on this floor protested. They have the right to do it, and we cannot take that right from them. They will exercise it. The people have the right to think, and they will exercise that right. They have the right of memorializing, and they will exercise that right. They have the right to express their opinions, and they will exercise that right. They will exercise their rights in reprobation or commendation at the ballot-box, too; and preachers, I believe, vote. They have the right to do so. They are not very formidable numerically, but they have the right to do this as ministers of the Gospel, as well as we Senators have a right to vote for the adoption of a measure; and if it is not in accordance with their opinions they have a right to condemn it. They have the right to think it is morally wrong, politically wrong, civilly wrong, and socially wrong, if they do not interfere with the vested rights of others in the entertainment of those opinions.

I understood my honorable friend from Mississippi to say that the South had been groaning for a long time under this oppressive measure. The South, sir, are a spirited people, and how they could have submitted for more than a third of a century to this indignity, this wrong, this act of oppression, which has ground them down in their prosperity and development, and never have said a word about it until this auspicious moment arrived, and that, too, when political subjects have been agitated at the north and south, that it should have been reserved for the action of the present Congress, after all others had glided by without complaint, rebuke, remonstrance, or suggestion of appeal, is a most extraordinary thing. My friend does not apprehend it; but there was no excitement out of this Capitol, or out of the city of Washington. It originated here. This was the grand laboratory of political action and political machinery. The object was to mature the measure here, and inflict it, by a *coup d'état*, upon the nation, and then radiate it to every point of the country. The potion does not react pleasantly. There is a response, but how does it go down? Not well. The physic works; it works badly; it works upward.

I am willing to receive any memorials that are presented to this body which are respectable in terms, whether they come from preachers, politicians, civilians, or from the beggars that congregate about your cities, and I will treat them with respect and kindness. As long as they are respectful in terms to this body, though they express their apprehension of a calamity about to fall on the country, it brands no man; and if they denounce a measure in advance, it is what they have a right to do. We have a more eligible position here to advocate our opinions than individuals have in social life to maintain their positions. We have all the panoply of power and State sovereignty thrown around the members of this body to guard and shield them against attacks; but they are thrown in the midst of the community without any shield except it is the shield of morality and propriety of conduct which gives protection to their person. While they express themselves respectfully, I shall never treat with disrespect preachers or any other individuals who come before this body to give us their opinions upon political subjects.

Mr. EVERETT. Mr. President, as this memorial was presented by me, I think it my duty to say a few words to the Senate by way of explaining my relations to it. Just after the Senate came to order this morning, I was called from my seat to the door of the Senate chamber, and there requested to take charge of it—this memorial. The gentleman in whose hands it was, with whom I had not the pleasure of a previous personal acquaintance, was introduced to me, as I have no doubt he is, a most respectable member of the clerical profession; and I was requested by him to take charge of the memorial and present it to the Senate. Seeing that it was a very voluminous document, and one which I could not carry with me to my seat, and there hand it, in the usual manner, to the attendants of the Senate, I directed one of them near me at the door to take it immediately to the table of the Secretary, so that I have had no opportunity whatever of inspecting it. I presented it to the Senate but a moment or two after it was placed in my charge, and, in point of fact, I had not read a word of it before I cast my eye over it and a few of the signatures at the head of it, in conjunction with the Senator from Illinois, the chairman of the Committee on the Territories, as we were standing together at the Secretary's table. I think it due to myself, as a matter of fact, that these circumstances should be stated, because the Senator from Illinois has objected to the language of the memorial, as disrespectful to the Senate, and as personally offensive to him, in common with the other members of the body who supported the bill. I am aware of the reserve which is imposed by the rules of the Senate on the presentation of memorials; and I deem it, therefore, no more than justice to myself that the Senate should understand precisely the circumstances under which this memorial was offered by me.

I think, however, sir, that I ought to go further, and, inasmuch as the time of its presentation is objected to, express, in justice to the memorialists, the opinion that this memorial was signed by probably every individual whose name is subscribed to it before the final action of the Senate on the Nebraska bill. It is probable, in collecting together the separated papers which had been circulated for signatures, and in preparing the memorial to be transmitted, in the copy of the caption which was made for that purpose, the date of the first of March was appended to it, without considering that many of the memorialists, probably all, must have signed it before that day. It ought not, therefore, to be considered, as has been complained of, as a protest directed against a measure which so large a majority of the Senate had previously sanctioned, but as the expression of the opinion entertained by those who signed it of a measure still pending before the Senate.

I do not undertake to vouch that this is the fact; but I presume that Senators will themselves, on reflection, consider that it must be so; and that the memorial must have been signed by a majority, if not by every individual whose name is there, while the measure was in its progress, and not after it had received the approbation of a great majority of this body.

My own opinion in relation to presenting memorials to the Senate in reference to measures that have passed from our control would be, that it is, generally speaking, not expedient. In a single instance of a memorial against the Nebraska bill, sent to me since the measure left this body, I have, at the suggestion of the person who sent it, instead of presenting it here, put it into the hands of the member of the other House who represents the district where the memorialists live. That was done at the request of the person who forwarded the memorial. Observing, however, that other Senators around me, in many cases, did present memorials which had reached them since the bill passed through the Senate, and contemplating the possibility that it might again come before us, after having undergone amendment in the other House, and that there was therefore still a propriety in its being considered, to a qualified extent, in our possession, I have thought there was no irregularity in that point of view, in presenting any memorial to which there was no objection on other grounds. On this principle I have acted in reference to several memorials against the Nebraska bill which have been sent to me during the past week.

In reference to the objections taken to the language of the memorial, and the concerted movement in which it has originated, I must say to the Senator from Illinois, that I do not believe there is anything in it intended for political effect. I have no belief that these three thousand clergymen from all parts of New England, in preparing and signing this memorial, have intended, in the smallest degree, to step from their sacred profession into the arena of party politics. I am confident it would be found, if it were possible to make the inquiry, that the memorial is signed by individuals of all political parties; that those who differ on every political question, in the common acceptation of the term, will be found to have united on this occasion; that this paper really expresses the sincere conviction of men who look at this subject strictly in a moral and religious aspect, and that, so far from designing to take any part in the agitations that trouble the land, they have regarded the question solely in the other point of view in which it is natural it should present itself to their minds.

This has, from time immemorial, been the custom of the members of that profession, in that part of the country, although not confined to it. They have been in the habit, in reference to public questions which have strongly appealed to the sensibilities of the community, and which they regarded as having momentous moral and religious bearings, of expressing their opinions in this way; and I am quite sure, as I said before, that on this occasion they have not intended to lay aside—they have not thought they were laying aside—their sacred character for the sake of joining in political agitation, or affecting the result of any political controversy. And, sir, I think I need not say, that a body of over three thousand clergymen, comprehending more than three fourths of the clerical profession of New England, of all denominations, is a very respectable body, that it must faithfully represent the public opinion of a very large and most intelligent portion of the community, and that it is entitled to the most respectful consideration on the part of this body. I do not wish, as a citizen myself of that part of the Union, to say any thing that would be thought extravagant, or dictated by local partiality or that point, but I must say that I do not think it would be possible to find any body of men of the same number embracing a greater amount of personal and moral worth than these three thousand and fifty individuals. The greater portion of them are necessarily men of education. They are persons whose lives are consecrated, with very little reward in what are called this world's goods, to the highest objects to which the life and labors of a man can be devoted. Of course, in such a large number of men, there may be individual exceptions, but I do think that, in general, it may be very fairly said they are as exemplary, as intelligent, and as respectable a body of men as any other in the country, not to say in the world; and I must repeat my conviction, that on this occasion they were animated by no desire to embark in the strife and agitation of the world of politics; but that feeling they were performing a duty that devolved upon them, they have expressed their honest and sincere conviction of the character of the measure in question, contemplated in a moral and religious point of view.

I regret that the presentation of this memorial, which, under the circumstances, I could regard in no other light than as a duty to a large number of my own immediate constituents, should have awakened any feelings on the part of any member of the Senate. It is but three or four days since my friend from New York [Mr. FISH] presented a similar memorial—I mean similar in its object, for I have had no opportunity of comparing the terms in which it is couched—subscribed by almost every clergyman in the city of New York. It was headed by the distinguished bishop of the eastern diocess of that State; and it was represented to be signed by a large majority of the clergy of that city. No exception was taken in the Senate to that memorial; none to its terms; none to the facts of the presentation. It was received in the usual form and ordered to lie upon the table in the usual manner. That, if I recollect right, was since the passage of the bill; and it took the course which other numerous memorials have taken which have also been presented since its passage. I think it would be wise and expedient that this memorial also should be received and disposed of in the usual way. I am quite sure that it would be doing injustice to the individuals who signed it, many of whom are personally known to me, as men venerable for years, distinguished for learning, and of the utmost purity of life and character, to reject their memorial as having been prompted by any desire to kindle angry passions, or to engage in political controversy; but that we ought to give them the credit for having expressed honestly and sincerely the feelings and opinions which they entertained of this measure as a moral and religious question.

I do not know, sir, that I have any thing more to say on this subject. I felt that it was due to the relation in which, without any previous intimation, I have been placed to the memorialists that I should say this much.

Mr. PETTIT. Mr. President, I am for the greatest liberty to the greatest number, and I will not deny to any class of my fellow citizens, under whatever name or denomination they may appear, the right to petition; and under the general term "petition," provided for in the Constitution, I am willing to regard memorials and remonstrances, of whatever name, kind, or description, provided always they are respectful to the Senate. But they should be viewed in another light, and that is as to the propriety of time.

Then the first objection which I make to this remonstrance is not to its terms, not to it of itself, but to the time of its presentation. All memorializing and all petitioning is upon the basis or hypothesis that some good is to come of it; that there is something pending, or likely to be pending, to which it may refer. In that view, it is certainly too late now to present this memorial, though, as for that, I care but little. The bill has passed from us, never to return to us, in all probability. We have done our deed, for good or for evil, for weal or for woe. We are to have, I suppose, the righteous judgments of the country and of the Almighty upon us for the doing of that deed. I presume this memorial intends to convey the idea, although it does not say so distinctly, that we subject ourselves to the righteous judgments of the Almighty, to judgments which are terrible and fearful, judgments of torment, of pain, and of misery. I will not, however, so construe it, for my own gratification at least. I am willing to say that the righteous judgments of the Almighty held in reserve for us are those of approval and reward. I doubt not that we shall receive, through the country, through our fellow-citizens, that judgment of reward and approval. The bill, however, to which this remonstrance relates, has passed from us, not to return. It has gone entirely to the other House, and I can see no propriety in piling upon our table remonstrances against the passage of a measure which we have already passed.

But, sir, the Senator from Mississippi [Mr. ADAMS] says he has great respect and great reverence for the clergy, for the ministers of the Gospel, as such, while they keep their robes pure and unspotted; but when they descend to the turbid pools of politics, and bedabble their garments all over with the mud, and slime, and filth which he would make you believe is to be found there, he loses all respect for them. So should I, if I could be led to believe that the waters of the pool of politics were any more turbid or filthy than the waters which flow through their contradictory streams of theology. I do not believe it, sir. I hold, on the contrary, that the waters of the pools of politics are infinitely more pelucid, and pure, and cheering, and refreshing, than the pool which surrounds their stagnant waters of theology—no two of them agreeing on any proposition which can be presented.

I am, however, totally incompetent to judge of this matter. These men, as has been well said by the Senator from Virginia, have not come to you as fellow-citizens. The Constitution has secured to the citizens of the United States the right at all times to petition, and they shall never be denied that right by me, whether they choose to use the name of citizens or any other. But they have not remonstrated in their own name as citizens, nor in behalf of their fellow-citizens; but they have come, as they tell you, as the ambassadors of a higher and an omnipotent power. They use the language of an ambassador who says, "in the name of my Government, I declare to you this, that, or the other." In the name of God, and in the name of his violated law, they declare this. They say that to them alone is given the power to divulge or to divine that law on earth. Sir, being totally incompetent, avowing here my total incapacity and inability to expound, divine, and illustrate that law, I shall leave it to a different forum and a different place.

These memorialists do not tell us that the measure against which they protest, will injure the country, or that it is a wrong to their fellow-citizens; but that it is a violation of the law of Him, their master, who, they claim, has sent them. The propriety of such a remonstrance may well be questioned; yet I will not undertake to question it.

Sir, this, then, is an ecclesiastical, not a political question. They have withdrawn it from the political arena. They have said that they are sent by the Divine Creator, the Maker and enforcer of divine law, commissioned to put forth and to thunder on our devoted heads his anathemas and his judgments in advance. As a secular body, we are entirely incompetent to judge of what that law is, or whether we have offended against it or not. These men say they are commissioned to expound it on earth to us. We have, however, provided ourselves for all these contingencies. When the people, in their political capacity, send their petitions or memorials here, they know we are competent to understand them, and to provide for their interests. But, sir, I suppose we have taken a step with a view of meeting the present condition of affairs. We have provided ourselves with a law officer of this law—an expounder of the divine law; a "brother" of the same class with those who now remonstrate; an officer of this body, who, from his age, his high standing, and many endorsements here, must be supposed to be as capable of expounding that law as any of these remonstrants. I think the fact that he has been selected by a body of such intelligence as the Senate, shows that he ought to be superior to any of them as an officer of that law which these men say we have violated and outraged. I will therefore suggest, at any rate, and I believe I shall propose, that this remonstrance be referred to the Rev. Henry Slicer, Chaplain of this Senate, for examination and report. [Laughter.]

Now, sir, I want to know whether the officer of the Senate whom we have elected and appointed to expound the divine law and the divine will to us, will, not upon any oath of office, but upon his responsibility as an officer of this body, after calmly and deliberately weighing our actions here with the whole tendency, bearing, and spirit of the revealed will of God, say to us that we have so violated it. If he will, I believe I shall be ready to retract my vote on the bill, and agree to adopt his report, and go to my colleagues in the other House, and ask them for God's sake to send back the bill here, in order that we may retract our steps.

This, I repeat, is an ecclesiastical question. We are threatened with the anathemas, the thunders of the Almighty against us for violating his law. As a secular body here, we are no judges of that law; but we have provided ourselves with one who is a judge of it; and to him I think this whole matter ought to be referred. I think it will be no disrespect to the memorialists or the petitioners if we do so. They claim that they are gentlemen of the cloth, preachers of the Gospel. Now, we have elected one, and he is here, who is a gentleman of the cloth, and a minister of the Gospel of long experience; and I should be exceedingly glad to have his official report on this question, as to whether we are in danger, whether we have invoked the just and righteous judgments of God upon us. Therefore, sir, if it is in order, I will move to refer the memorial to the Rev. Henry Slicer, the Chaplain of the Senate. [Laughter.]

Mr. DOUGLAS. So far as I am concerned, I am willing that the memorial shall be allowed to lie upon the table. The reason why I called attention to it at all was this: I have seen a deliberate attempt to organize the clergy of this country into a great political sectional party for Abolition schemes. That project was put forth clearly in the Abolition manifesto which I had to expose in my opening speech upon the Nebraska bill. This is a response to that Abolition manifesto. It is an attempt to give in the adhesion of the religious societies of this country through the clergy to the Abolition and political schemes of that organization. If these preachers choose to go into that political organization it is not for me to object, provided they confine their operations to the country, and do not send their insults here. I have no idea that these men would ever have dreamt of bringing forward such an objectionable document as this, but in response to that call which emanated from the Senate. It was by Senators in their official capacity as Senators, and these remonstrances have been sent back in response to the call.

Now, sir, what is this remonstrance? These men do not protest as citizens. They do not protest in the name either of themselves or of their fellow-citizens. They do not even protest *in their own* names as clergymen, against this act, but they say that 'WE PROTEST IN THE NAME OF ALMIGHTY GOD;' and in order to make it more emphatic that they claim to speak by authority in their remonstrance, they underscore in broad black lines the words 'IN THE NAME OF ALMIGHTY GOD.' It is true they describe themselves as ministers of the Gospel, but they claim to speak in the name of the Almighty upon a political question pending in the Congress of the United States. It is an attempt to establish in this country the doctrine that a body of men organized and known among the people as clergymen, have a peculiar right to determine the will of God in relation to legislative action. It is an attempt to establish a theocracy to take charge of our politics and our legislation. It is an attempt to make the legislative power of this country subordinate to the church. It is not only to unite Church and State, but it is to put the State in subordination to the dictates of the church. Sir, you cannot find in the most despotic countries, in the darkest ages, a bolder attempt on the part of the ministers of the Gospel to usurp the power of Government, and to say to the people: "You must not think for yourselves; you must not dare to act for yourselves; you must in all matters pertaining to the affairs of this life, as well as the next, receive instructions from us; and that, too, in the performance of your civil and official, as well as your religious duties."

Sir, I called attention to this matter for the purpose of showing that it involved a great principle subversive of our free institutions. If we recognize three thousand clergymen as having a higher right to interpret the will of God than we have, we destroy the right of self-action, of self-government, of self-thought, and we are merely to refer each of our political questions to this body of clergymen to inquire of them whether it is in conformity with the law of God and the will of the Almighty or not. This document, I repeat, purports to speak in the name of Almighty God, and then enters a protest in that name. We are put under the ban, we are excommunicated, the gates of Heaven are closed unless we obey this behest and stop in our course and carry out these Abolition views.

The Senator from Texas says the people have a right to petition. I do not question it. I do not wish to deprive ministers of the Gospel of that right. I do not acknowledge that there is any member of this body who has a higher respect and veneration either for a minister of the Gospel or for his holy calling than I have; but my respect is for him *in his calling*. I will not controvert what the Senator from Massachusetts has said as to there being, perhaps, no body of men in this country, three thousand in number, who combine more respectability than these clergymen. Probably they combine all the respectability which he claims for them; but I will add, that I doubt whether there is a body of men in America who combine so much profound ignorance on the question upon which they attempt to enlighten the Senate, as this same body of preachers. How many of them, do you suppose sir, have ever taken up and read the act of 1820 to which I allude? Do you think there is one of them who has done so? How many of them ever read the votes by which the North repudiated that act of 1820? Do you think one of them ever did? How many of them ever read the various votes which I quoted on that act and the Arkansas act? Do you think one of them knew any thing about them? How many of them have ever traced the course of the compromise measures of 1850 on the record? One of them? Yet they assume, in the name of the Almighty, to judge of facts, and laws, and votes, of which they know nothing, and which they have no time to understand, if they perform their duties as clergymen to their respective flocks.

They do not pretend to judge from the knowledge of this world, from the records of the Senate, or from the statute-book, or from any of the sources of information on which Senators and citizens predicate their action; but by the will and the law of God, and in his name, and in consequence of their divine mission, they overrule all these and prescribe a new test, and, in that name, they tell us that by the passage of the bill which we have passed, we have committed a moral wrong. They tell us that it is subversive of all confidence in national engagements.

Now, let me ask, are these men particularly tenacious of national engagements? Did they in their pulpits, in 1850 and 1851, tell their followers that they were bound by their oaths, and by their religious duty, to surrender fugitive slaves in obedience to the constitution? Did they then tell their people that they must perform national engagements? Did they then tell their flocks that the Senate was right in carrying out the provisions of the constitution? Have they been particularly in the habit of enjoining in the pulpit and from the sacred desk, as a matter of conscience, that the people should perform the national engagements contained in the constitution of our country, and which we are all sworn to support? Sir, I do not remember that any one of these three thousand preachers, at the time when in Boston and other points of this country there were attempts to resist the fugitive slave law by force, came forward and said it was a divine duty to perform national engagements. If they did, I have not seen the evidence of it. If they felt it was a matter of conscience and of duty on the part of the clergy to supervise the fulfilment of national engagements, to preserve the public faith, and the public honor, where were they then, when your constitution was trampled upon, when oaths of office could not bind men to perform their constitutional duty, when public honor was being outraged? Where then were these three thousand clergymen? We did not hear from them on that occasion. There was a national engagement which no man can deny; yet they did not raise their voices against its violation. But in this case, merely because some Abolitionists from this body have said that an act of Congress constituted a national engagement, although the statement is contradicted by the record, they come forward at the bidding of an abolition *junta*, to arraign the Senate of the United States in the name of the Almighty!

Sir, I deny their authority. I deny that they have any such commission from the Almighty to decide this question. I deny that our constitution confers any such right upon them. I deny that the Bible confers any such right upon them. They can perform their duties within their sphere without my censure or my interference, and they are responsible to the Almighty for the manner in which they perform those duties; and I must be left to perform my duties within the sphere of my functions, with no other responsibility than to my constituents and to the Almighty, without the interference of those men. I do not acknowledge them as an intermediate tribunal.

I do not acknowledge that they are, as the gentleman from Texas has called them, the vicegerents of the Almighty, and that they are to perform the duty of overlooking our conduct. I repudiate the whole doctrine as at war with the pure principles of Christianity, at war with the spirit of our institutions, at war with our constitution, at war with every principle upon which a free government can rest.

Then, sir, assuming this character, they come forward and tell us that the action of the Senate exposes us to the "righteous judgments of the Almighty." Their leaders here try to avoid the force of the objection that this is offensive, upon the ground that the Senate had not voted upon the question at the time when the memorial was signed. However the fact may be as to the time of signing the protest, it cannot be denied that they sent it here for presentation by their own agent more than one week after the vote of the Senate had been published to the world. This excuse does not avail them, nor exculpate their conduct. It only furnishes evidence that their apologists here have become ashamed of their conduct. I wish it distinctly understood that I attach no blame to the Senator from Massachusetts, [Mr. EVERETT,] who presented this document, for his uniform conduct has proven him incapable of performing an improper act here knowingly. His explanation has set him right. But the fact still remains that this offensive protest has been sent here and presented to the Senate as an impeachment of our conduct in passing a bill which received the sanction of this body by a vote of 37 yeas to 14 nays.

But, passing that by, if it is not offensive to the Senate, because the Senate had not voted on the bill at the time, it was offensive to the Committee on Territories, who had reported it, and it is as much a violation of the rules of the Senate, of courtesy, and of decency, to bring in a document which is offensive to one of your committees, as to bring in one which is offensive to the body itself. Then that excuse will not avail.

Individually, I care nothing about this matter. To me it is a very small affair, compared with the sort of treatment which I am receiving every day. I submit to it with great composure. I wait for the coming of the day when the people will understand the real principle involved in the Nebraska bill. Sir, I hope to see the day arrive—surely it will arrive—when you will not be able to find a man in the United States who will acknowledge that he was ever opposed to that great principle of self-government, unless you can pin him by the record, and then he will have some excuse on some immaterial point. These confederates can have their triumph now, by heaping on our heads insult and calumny, and by deceiving even ministers of the Gospel and members of churches into acts of excess which are disgraceful to them and of which they will be ashamed when the question comes to be fairly understood.

And, sir, when that revolution comes, when that revulsion of feeling from an indignant people who have been misled under holy pretences for base partisan purposes, returns upon them, I then will be able to say, "Now you get the reward of your own conduct." I bide my time; I take no exception to what is going on now, but I wish to enter my protest against the Senate giving its sanction to the recognition of the clergy of this country as a body of men authorized to judge upon political and legislative questions in the name of the Almighty, and without any responsibility to the people. It reverses the whole principle of our Government, and it was only to enter my protest against that reversal that I called the attention of the Senate to this protest.

Mr. HOUSTON. Mr. President, as the honorable Senator from Illinois, the chairman of the Committee on Territories, seemed in a most emphatic manner to address his remarks to me, I think him fully entitled to the respect of my attention. He has dwelt upon the Abolition character of this document. So far as any such character may be embodied in it, I have nothing to say. There are various opinions entertained here and elsewhere upon various subjects with which I have nothing to do, and with which I have no affiliation; but with this subject, as it is presented to the Senate now, I have some connection. With the controversy which exists between the honorable chairman of the Committee on Territories and the gentleman from Ohio, [Mr. CHASE,] and the gentleman from Massachusetts, [Mr. SUMNER,] I have nothing to do. I was not here when the controversy originated, nor when it was first introduced into the Senate. I have not participated in it since; and however unpleasant such altercations or controversies may be, and however I may regard them as impeding the transaction of business in this body, I have forborne either public or private expressions of opinion upon that matter.

Mr. DOUGLAS. Mr. President, I will say to the Senator that the only allusion which I had to him was the simple quotation which I made from his remarks when he spoke of these ministers being the vicegerents of the Almighty. My other remarks were intended for another quarter, so far as they had an application anywhere. If he is under the misapprehension of supposing that they referred to him, I wish to correct him; that is all. I do not want to interrupt him.

Mr. HOUSTON. I am very glad to hear the disclaimer, for the gentleman's remarks appeared to be directed so unequivocally toward me that I was led into the misapprehension of supposing that they were intended perhaps to apply to me, in a manner in which it was not the purpose of the gentleman to apply them. But, sir, I explained when I was up before, the misapplication of the term "vicegerent," and I expressed my opinion to be that the ministers of the Gospel were the heralds of the Almighty God, or his ministers of peace upon earth. I thought the gentleman would not have carped upon that expression unless with reference to some particular influence which my views might have upon the auditory. It was a mere misapplication of a term, and I so explained it.

But, Mr. President, I think the object of this memorial is misapprehended. I find no fault with its introduction, either before or after the passage of the bill to which it refers, for that bill may be returned to the Senate with amendments. Such things very frequently occur. At all events, as the memorial has been prepared with great care, and as the gentlemen who have signed it have been anxious that their views should be laid before the Senate of the United States, lest other measures embracing similar principles should be introduced, I can see nothing improper in allowing them to lay their views respectfully before the Senate. I do not think there is any evidence that the gentlemen who have signed the memorial have any disposition to establish theocracy in our country, or that they wish to take the Government into their own hands and exercise a controlling influence over it. We find that those who have signed this document are of different sects and various denominations. I think there is no danger that such an amalgamation of interests and opinions will take place as to embody a force sufficient to make any great impression on the institutions of this country, or to endanger our liberties.

Mr. President, this memorial is regarded as a substantive and independent matter, as intended to produce agitation and to insult the Senate; but it is really the effect of a measure which I predicted would have this influence upon the community. The cause exists in the Senate. It exists in the amendment inserted into the Nebraska bill proposing the repeal of the Missouri compromise, and this is but responsive action to that. The cause is not in the clergymen who have signed this memorial. The memorial is the effect of a cause brought forward and presented in the Senate. The memorial impugns the action of no one. It is true, the memorialists speak of the measure as immoral. Surely that ought not to insult Senators. They are not such paragons of morality that they cannot bear to have their moral character questioned, if they should happen to do anything which would not be strictly moral according to some standards, but which I should not think to be very immoral. But is their morality of such a delicate texture as to be affected by a memorial coming from "the land of steady habits?"

We are told that there is a great principle involved in the bill to which this memorial refers. This is a very formidable and very visible response to that great principle which it is said has lain dormant. Sir, I need not name the number of years that it has lain dormant. No bright genius ever elicited it; no brilliant conception ever discovered it until this session had progressed for some time, when the great principle of non-intervention at once sprang up to illumine the world, to be regarded as one which, at some future day, would be a universally-recognized principle. Sir, I recognize the principles of self-government, but I do it in sovereignty. A people in tutelage cannot exercise sovereignty, but States can. A people who are in a territorial existence, which is fitting them to become States, exercise what may be called a *quasi* sovereignty. They are never really sovereign until they are recognized by Congress as such, and are received into the Union as sovereign States. Then is the time for the operation of self-government, but it grows out of sovereignty. Is it to be in five squatters? They may pass a law to-day and repeal it to-morrow, and the next day they may pass another law, and so on successively from day to day and from year to year they may pass and repeal laws. The Territories have no power to pass organic laws until the attributes of sovereignty are about to attach, or have actually attached to them. That is what I call non-intervention. That is what I call sovereignty and self-government.

This is the great principle which it is said is involved in the bill which we have passed; and now we are receiving the response to it. I hope we may never have any more responses of this description. I pray heaven that we may never have another such protest in this body. I pray that there may never exist any necessity for it. But for the necessity or cause, which originated in this body, this memorial would never have been laid upon your table. This is but the effect; the cause was anterior to it. If we wish to avert calamitous effects, we should prevent pernicious causes.

Mr. SEWARD. Mr. President, I do not intend to be drawn, by any remarks which have been made, into a discussion of the question which was so elaborately discussed and finally disposed of, so far as this House is concerned, the week before last; but I have a few words to say upon the mere incident, the circumstance which, happening here this morning, is the subject of discussion. I understand that the honorable Senator from Virginia, [Mr. Mason,] who moved that this petition should not be received, submitted that motion after the petition, in fact, had been received; and therefore I suppose that motion is not in order, and will not be insisted upon. I do not understand the honorable Senator from Indiana [Mr. Pettit] seriously to propose to refer to the chaplain of the Senate a paper addressed to the Senate for its consideration.

Mr. PETTIT. If our rules allow it, I shall insist on that reference.

Mr. SEWARD. I understand the honorable Senator to assume that the rules do not allow it, and that it therefore cannot be done. Hence I will address no remarks to the Senate on that point. I understand the honorable Senator from Illinois, [Mr. Douglas,] who objected to this memorial, to say that, after having delivered his sentiments on the subject of the measure to which it referred, he, for one, would consent that the memorial should lie on the table. That is precisely what is desired by the petitioners themselves, or those who represent them here on this occasion. I understand, therefore, that there is no legislative question before the Senate at all in regard to this matter; but that practically we are all agreed that this memorial or petition, respectful or otherwise, right or wrong, shall lie on the table. Then I understand the design of the honorable Senator from Illinois, and of those who have addressed the Senate upon this occasion, has been to reply to the remarks which are contained in the memorial upon the subject of the Nebraska bill, and the abrogation of the Missouri compromise. Though I do not think this is a customary, or a right way to meet memorials or remonstrances from the people, yet, inasmuch as several Senators from different parts of the country have thought it proper to reply, by the expression of their opinions and sentiments, upon the propriety of this memorial, and the propriety of those who have sent it here, I barely wish to state for myself what I think on the subject.

Now, Mr. President, I have to say, in the first place, that if the presentation of this memorial here is wrong at all, it is wrong either in regard to the time, or the place or the circumstance, or the character of the memorialists, or the argument which the memorial makes.

Well, sir, I think those who will reflect on the subject will see that there is no censure justly to be cast upon the memorialists in regard to the time. It has been the habitual practice of the Senate to receive memorials and petitions upon subjects which were not yet before the body for action, and might never be; as, for instance, memorials upon the subject of securing the liberty of conscience to American citizens in foreign countries, have been received without question. So in regard to this matter. It is a subject which is one of legitimate consideration for the Senate. Although the Senate have acted on it, their action is as yet inchoate; it is liable to be reviewed directly. When the bill shall pass the other House, if ever, it may and probably will come back to us with amendments. Even if this were not so, still the Senate might be convinced, by the arguments of the memorialists or otherwise, that they had acted unwisely and injuriously to the country. If so, it is not too late to rescind our action. We can take measures to repeal the act if it shall ever pass.

Then, sir, in regard to the character of the persons who have presented this memorial; is there anything wrong in that? It is said they are clergymen, but they are nevertheless American citizens, and the broader qualification of citizenship covers over the lesser and inferior character and description of clergymen. Every man who is a citizen of the United States, and, according to my theory, every man who, although he may not be a citizen, yet is a subject of the Government of the United States, has a right to petition the Congress of the United States upon any subject of national interest, or which can be legitimately the subject of legislation. Then, is there any well-grounded objection to the fact that they describe themselves as clergymen? Certainly not; because it is the right and the privilege of a citizen, if he can petition at all, to present his petition in his own way. If he thinks there is anything in his character or position which entitles his opinions to higher consideration, or which leads to the belief that he understands the subject more thoroughly than others, it is his right to describe himself by the appellation which designates his profession, his character, or his office. It is only on this principle that the Legislatures of the States make their voices known to Congress, by describing themselves as the Legislatures of the States. After all, they come here with their resolutions in the character of petitioners or remonstrants, under that provision of the constitution which guarantees the right of petition, and upon no other ground of constitutional right whatever.

Is there, then, any well-gounded objection to the language or tone of this memorial? I think not. While, on the other hand, it is such a memorial as a secular person like myself would not be apt to dictate or sign, because there is a solemnity of tone, a seriousness, and religious consideration which secular men do not indulge or affect; yet, on the other hand, it is professional, and natural on the part of the memorialists; it is in the character of those who make it. It is said, indeed, that they assume to speak the will, and judgment, and pleasure of the Creator, and judge of men and nations. I do not understand them as assuming to speak any such thing. I understand them as saying simply, in substance, "We, citizens of the United States, subscribing ourselves as clergymen in the presence of Almighty God, and in His name, address the Congress of the United States." Sir, what is unusual or wrong in this? You do not commence your proceedings here on any day of your whole session without acknowledging and declaring that they are begun in the presence, and in the name, and with an invocation of the blessing of Almighty God.

Mr. MASON. Will the Senator allow me to interrupt him for a moment.

Mr. SEWARD. Certainly.

Mr. MASON. If the Senator will look at the memorial, he will find that the signers carefully exclude their character of citizens. They speak of themselves as clergymen of the United States in the name of Almighty God, and in his presence making this protest before the Senate.

Mr. SEWARD. I may agree with the honorable Senator as to the fact that they do not state their citizenship, or their character as citizens; but I believe there is no dispute of the fact that they are citizens of the United States.

Mr. MASON. *Non constat.*

Mr. SEWARD. I say that is so. It is practically known to us that the clergy of this country are persons who are invested with the rights of citizens. I have said, sir, that they come here declaring that they come in the presence of Almighty God. It is that universal and eternal presence in which we all are every day and hour of our lives, and from which we can never for even a moment escape.

Again, sir, it is objected that they say they address us in the name of Almighty God. What is that but a mode of arresting or calling attention to their solemn prayer and earnest remonstrance? Sir, while there are occasions on which we never forget, never suffer ourselves to forget that we are responsible to Almighty God, it is equally true that all our action is, or ought to be, in the name of the Supreme Being. Sir, we may put off, we may lay aside the thoughts of that awful presence during our secular labors and during our life of confusion and toil and turmoil and care; but when we come to close our eyes upon this world, we cannot shut them without the reflection that we are ever here in the sight of the Judge of all men. Every man of us, when he comes to write his opinion, or his will, or his instructions for those who are to come after him, recites that it is done in the name of God. Sir, as I have said, I should not adopt this mode of addressing the Senate or Congress. It is not my habit to do so; but I know that it is the habit, that it is in the character, in the way of those who have signed this memorial. I see no ground of objection to it. Is it disrespectful to the Senate of the United States, or to Congress, that men should say they speak to them in the name of God, and in his presence? If it be so, it must be because we claim to be here exempt from the superintending government and providence of that Being, in whom and by whom we live and walk, and through whom we exist upon the earth.

But, sir, it is said that at the close of this remonstrance, there is another remark which is offensive, and that is, that the memorialists think the measure against which they protest is immoral in its nature, and that among its consequences it will draw down upon us—not upon this Senate, but upon the nation, upon this people—the judgments of Almighty God. Sir, the *question* in the great measure proposed is either moral or immoral. There is no neutrality between morality and immorality. It may be that we may conscientiously differ in ascertaining which is the moral side, but nevertheless it is of one character or the other—either moral or immoral. These persons tell us they think it is of one character, others think it is of another character. It is our right to act. Let them think what they will, it is their right to tell us that, in their opinion, it is either one thing or the other, just as they understand and believe.

Then, again, it is said that the memorialists allege that the act will draw after it the judgments of Almighty God. Sir, by the judgments of Almighty God, I understand simply this: that every human act of any importance or magnitude is connected with preceding causes, and with subsequent effects; that there is connected with a right act the consequence of usefulness, of beneficence, of happiness, and all the blessings of a just Ruler; and that, on the other hand, to those acts which, whether we deem them moral or immoral, whether intentionally wrong or not, are unwise, there are connected consequences of error, danger, peril, unhappiness, wretchedness, ruin. This, in my judgment, is all that that expression means.

Mr. BUTLER. I wish to bring one thing to the view of the honorable Senator, if he will allow me. I wish to ask whether it is his opinion, from any inspection of the paper, that the clergymen who signed it had the memorial before them at the time when they signed it? It purports to have been signed on the first of March, and the bill passed the Senate on the third of March. Will he tell me whether they did or did not sign their names blindly, without seeing the memorial?

Mr. SEWARD. The honorable Senator will excuse me from answering his question; for I have not gone nearer to the paper to look at it than I am now when I stand at my desk.

Mr. BUTLER. I venture to say they never saw the memorial. They could not have done it.

Mr. SEWARD. I was simply saying that these persons, being clergymen, being devoted to the worship of God and the cure of souls, have a language of their own, and that in this language they have expressed and embodied their opinions on a secular question, and that in it there is nothing which, by just construction, ought to give offence.

And now, sir, I come to the close of what I have to say on this whole matter; and that is, that I regard this as a question of no idle importance. The right of petition is a constitutional right, and a useful and invaluable one, and I shall never be found criticising the language of petitioners or remonstrants, to see whether I cannot find cause for cavil or for rejection. The petitioners and remonstrants may say precisely what they please, and precisely what they think, in whatever tone or language they think proper. They may use, for me, any epithet which they please. They may invoke on my head any judgment they please. Still, sir, with a conscience void of offence against God and man, I can go on here performing my duties, leaving them in the enjoyment of their rights, and listening to all that they say, precisely as if it had been rendered into the language of courtesy, or compliment, or of praise, which would be acceptable under other circumstances. It is because I wish that this right of petition may take no injury from the debate of this morning, that I have risen to vindicate the memorial, and to do justice to those from whom it has come.

Mr. BADGER. Mr. President, I think we have given rather more importance to the memorial than its intrinsic merits entitle it to. I have no doubt at all that what is said by my honorable friend from Massachusetts [Mr. EVERETT] is strictly true, that the gentlemen who have signed this paper belong to a class of highly respectable and excellent men. I would say, probably, with regard to each of them, what Sir Walter Scott, in one of his novels, makes Cromwell say in regard to the

Rev. Mr. Oldenough: "Lack-a-day, lack-a-day, a learned man, but intemperate; over-zeal hath eaten him up."

These gentlemen do not come here in the character of petitioners. These gentlemen do not come here in the character of remonstrants. They do not come here in the character of memorialists; but they come as protestors, not in their own name, not with the individual weight and authority which might be attributed to their protest on the ground of their own intelligence or worth, not merely with the weight and authority which might be superadded to this and other considerations from the fact of their being ministers of the Gospel. It is impossible to look at this paper without seeing that the honorable Senator from New York has specially pleaded upon the subject, and that the reverend gentlemen who signed it will not thank him for assigning them in this paper the low position in which he wishes to place them. What is it?

"The undersigned clergymen of different religious denominations in New England, hereby, in the name of Almighty God, solemnly protest."

In their official characters as ministers of Almighty God, and in his name, they protest against the passage of the Nebraska bill.

Now, sir, these are educated gentlemen. They are men of experience in their vocation. They understand the true and solemn import of the words here used; and I have not the shadow of a doubt that they meant to enter a protest, as the language imports, as a protest, through them, of the Almighty God himself, speaking to this Senate. It is not an expression preparatory to a solemn act to be done by them; for all that is completed when they declare that they speak in the presence of God—that is to say, with a solemn recollection of His presence, realizing His superintendence over what they are doing. What, then, do they mean, when they add that they speak in His name, unless it is that they speak by His authority? That can admit of no doubt.

Well, then, sir, the whole paper proceeds in the same name and by the same authority; and, among other things, they protest against the measure as a great moral wrong, a breach of faith eminently injurious to the moral principles of the community, subversive of all confidence in national engagements, and as exposing us to the righteous judgments of the Almighty. All that is announced by these gentlemen, as ministers of God, affecting to speak in His name.

The interpretation of the paper, sir, I think it is impossible to mistake; but I have said that I think too much importance, decidedly too much importance has been attached to it. Whether this is to be understood as a denunciation of the judgments of God, or as a prediction of his judgments, I deny the authority to denounce, and I deny the gift of prophecy, and, therefore, I think we need not have troubled ourselves further on the subject.

Each of these reverend gentlemen being in the habit, in his vocation and in his particular department, of ruling and governing his congregation, gets habitually, of course, the habit of speaking on all occasions with authority. I believe that they meant it as speaking by authority. I believe they thought they had authority for what they said, and that there was nothing improper in extending that authoritative style of speaking, in the name of the Master whose ministers they are, to the Senate, as they are in the habit of doing in their ordinary ministrations to the congregations who acknowledge them as pastors. But why should that disturb us? Who cares for it? Does any body believe they have power to hurl the thunder bolts of heaven? Does any man believe that they are gifted with the spirit of prophecy, and able to announce to us what, in the future course of things, will come to pass? Not at all. I dare say they are very good men, but, like the Rev. Mr. Oldenough, over zealous; and there, for one, I am willing to leave the subject. I move, then, that the memorial lie upon the table.

The motion was agreed to.

www.ingramcontent.com/pod-product-compliance
Lightning Source LLC
LaVergne TN
LVHW020643110826
845149LV00004B/1331

9781418190217